Minnesota Ecoregions

- Northern Glaciated Plains
- Northern Minnesota Wetlands
- Driftless Area
- Northern Lakes and Forests
- Northern Glaciated Plains
- Western Corn Belt Plains
- Lake Agassiz Plain

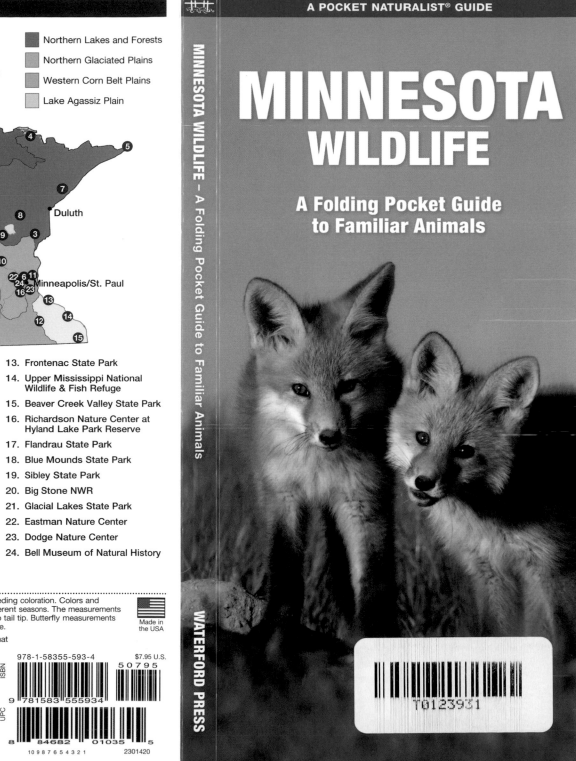

Duluth

Minneapolis/St. Paul

1. Agassiz National Wildlife Refuge (NWR)
2. MSU Regional Science Center
3. Audubon Center of the North Woods
4. Voyageurs National Park
5. Grand Portage State Park
6. Gooseberry Falls State Park
7. Rice Lake NWR
8. Mille Lacs Kathio State Park
9. Sherburne NWR
10. Tamarack Nature Center
11. Cascade Meadow Wetlands & Environmental Science Center
12. Frontenac State Park
13. Upper Mississippi National Wildlife & Fish Refuge
14. Beaver Creek Valley State Park
15. Richardson Nature Center at Hyland Lake Park Reserve
16. Flandrau State Park
17. Blue Mounds State Park
18. Sibley State Park
19. Big Stone NWR
20. Glacial Lakes State Park
21. Eastman Nature Center
22. Dodge Nature Center
23. Bell Museum of Natural History

Waterford Press publishes reference guides that introduce readers to nature observation, outdoor recreation and survival skills. Product information is featured on the website: www.waterfordpress.com

ISBN 978-1-58355-593-4 $7.95 U.S.

Made in the USA

2301420

A POCKET NATURALIST® GUIDE

MINNESOTA WILDLIFE – A Folding Pocket Guide to Familiar Animals

WATERFORD PRESS

MINNESOTA WILDLIFE

A Folding Pocket Guide to Familiar Animals

BUTTERFLIES

Black Swallowtail
Papilio polyxenes
To 3.5 in. (9 cm)

Cabbage White
Pieris rapae
To 2 in. (5 cm)
One of the most common butterflies.

Eastern Tiger Swallowtail
Papilio glaucus
To 6 in. (15 cm)

Orange Sulphur
Colias eurytheme
To 2.5 in. (6 cm)

Spring Azure
Celastrina ladon
To 1.25 in. (3.2 cm)
One of the earliest spring butterflies.

Eastern Tailed Blue
Cupido comyntas
To 1 in. (3 cm)
Note orange spots above thread-like hindwing "tails."

Underwings

Silver-spotted Skipper
Epargyreus clarus
To 2.5 in. (6 cm)
Has a large, irregular silver patch on the underside of its hindwings.

Monarch
Danaus plexippus
To 4 in. (10 cm)
Note rows of white spots on edges of wings.
Minnesota's state butterfly.

Viceroy
Limenitis archippus
To 3 in. (8 cm)
Told from similar monarch by its smaller size and the thin, black band on its hindwings.

Red Admiral
Vanessa atalanta
To 2.5 in. (6 cm)

Painted Lady
Vanessa cardui
To 2.5 in. (6 cm)

Great Spangled Fritillary
Speyeria cybele
To 3 in. (8 cm)
Common in marshes and wet meadows.

Eastern Comma
Polygonia comma
To 2 in. (5 cm)
Has a silvery comma mark on the underside of its hindwings.

Buckeye
Junonia coenia
To 2.5 in. (6 cm)
Note orange wing bars on forewings and eight distinct "eyespots."

White Admiral
Limenitis arthemis arthemis
To 3 in. (8 cm)

INVERTEBRATES

Bumble Bee
Bombus spp.
To 1 in. (3 cm)
Stout, furry bee is large and noisy. Can sting repeatedly.

Paper Wasp
Polistes spp.
To 1 in. (3 cm)
Builds papery hanging nests. Can sting repeatedly.

Honey Bee
Apis mellifera
To .75 in. (2 cm)
Slender bee has pollen baskets on its rear legs. Can only sting once.

Ladybug Beetle
Family Coccinellidae
To .5 in. (1.3 cm)
Red wing covers are black-spotted.

Green Darner
Anax junius
To 3 in. (8 cm)
Has blue to green thorax. Rests with its wings held open.

Black Horse Fly
Tabanus atratus
To 1.25 in. (3.2 cm)
Note large head. Females feed on blood and deliver painful bites. Similar deerflies have dark-patterned wings.

Ebony Jewelwing
Calopteryx maculata
To 2 in. (5 cm)

Yellow Jacket
Vespula spp.
To .5 in. (1.3 cm)
Picnic pest can sting repeatedly.

Twelve-spotted Skimmer
Libellula pulchella
To 2 in. (5 cm)

Field Cricket
Gryllus pennsylvanicus
To 1 in. (3 cm)
Shrill call is a series of 3 chirps.

True Katydid
Pterophylla camellifolia
To 2 in. (5 cm)
Loud 2-part call – katy-DID – is heard on summer evenings.

Annual Cicada
Tibicen canicularis
To 1.3 in. (3.5 cm)
Song is a sudden loud whine or buzz, maintained steadily before dying away.

Migratory Grasshopper
Melanoplus sanguinipes
To 1.5 in. (4 cm)

Black Widow Spider
Latrodectus mactans
To .3 in. (8 mm)
Black, shiny, bulbous abdomen has a red hourglass marking. Venom can be lethal to children.

Deer Tick
Ixodes scapularis
To .25 in. (.6 cm)
Feeds on the blood of mammals and can transmit disease-causing organisms between hosts.

Black-and-yellow Garden Spider
Argiope aurantia
To 1.25 in. (3.2 cm)

SPORT FISHES

Lake Whitefish
Coregonus clupeaformis
To 30 in. (75 cm)
Note concave forehead.

Brown Trout
Salmo trutta To 40 in. (1 m)
Has red and black spots on its body.

Brook Trout
Salvelinus fontinalis To 28 in. (70 cm)
Reddish side spots have blue halos.

Lake Trout
Salvelinus namaycush To 4 ft. (1.2 m)
Dark fish is covered in light spots. Tail is deeply forked.

Rainbow Trout
Oncorhynchus mykiss To 44 in. (1.1 m)
Note reddish side stripe.

Bluegill
Lepomis macrochirus To 16 in. (40 cm)

Pumpkinseed
Lepomis gibbosus To 16 in. (40 cm)

Walleye
Sander vitreus To 40 in. (1 m)
Note white spot on lower lobe of tail.
Minnesota's state fish.

Black Crappie
Pomoxis nigromaculatus To 16 in. (40 cm)

Muskellunge
Esox masquinongy To 6 ft. (1.8 m)

Smallmouth Bass
Micropterus dolomieu To 27 in. (68 cm)
Jaw joint is beneath the eye.

Northern Pike
Esox lucius To 53 in. (1.4 m)
Note large head and posterior dorsal fin.

Largemouth Bass
Micropterus salmoides To 40 in. (1 m)
Jaw joint extends beyond the eye.

Channel Catfish
Ictalurus punctatus To 4 ft. (1.2 m)

REPTILES & AMPHIBIANS

Chorus Frog
Pseudacris triseriata
To 1.5 in. (4 cm)
Note dark stripes on back. Call sounds like running a thumbnail over the teeth of a comb.

American Toad
Anaxyrus americanus
To 4.5 in. (11 cm)
Call is a high musical trill lasting up to 30 seconds.

Northern Leopard Frog
Lithobates pipiens
To 4 in. (10 cm)
Brown to green frog has dark spots on its back. Call is a rattling snore.

Wood Frog
Lithobates sylvaticus
To 3 in. (8 cm)
Note dark mask. Staccato call is duck-like.

Gray Treefrog
Hyla versicolor
To 2.5 in. (6 cm)
Call is a strong, resonating trill.

Snapping Turtle
Chelydra serpentina To 18 in. (45 cm)
Note knobby shell and long tail.

Tiger Salamander
Ambystoma tigrinum To 7 in. (18 cm)
Pattern of yellowish and dark blotches is variable.

Five-lined Skink
Plestiodon fasciatus To 8 in. (20 cm)
Has 5 light dorsal stripes.

Western Painted Turtle
Chrysemys picta bellii To 10 in. (25 cm)

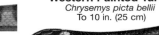
Northern Water Snake
Nerodia sipedon To 4.5 ft. (1.4 m)
Note dark blotches on back.

Ringneck Snake
Diadophis punctatus To 30 in. (75 cm)

Common Garter Snake
Thamnophis sirtalis To 4 ft. (1.2 m)
Green, brown or black snake has yellowish back stripes.

Smooth Green Snake
Opheodrys vernalis To 26 in. (65 cm)

Plains Garter Snake
Thamnophis radix To 40 in. (1 m)

Timber Rattlesnake
Crotalus horridus To 6 ft. (1.8 m)

Red-bellied Snake
Storeria occipitomaculata
To 16 in. (40 cm)
Brown to black snake has a light collar formed by 3 spots.

BIRDS

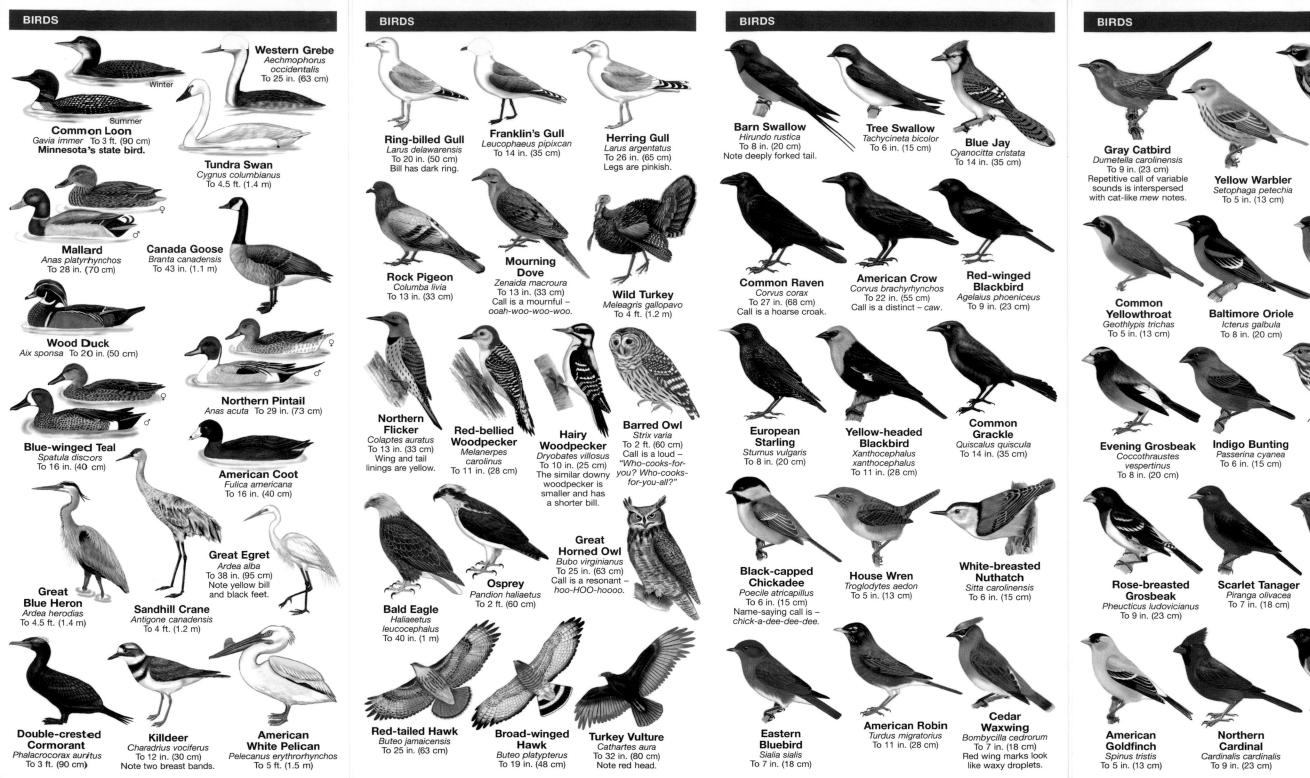

Western Grebe
Aechmophorus occidentalis
To 25 in. (63 cm)

Winter
Summer

Common Loon
Gavia immer To 3 ft. (90 cm)
Minnesota's state bird.

Tundra Swan
Cygnus columbianus
To 4.5 ft. (1.4 m)

Mallard
Anas platyrhynchos
To 28 in. (70 cm)

Canada Goose
Branta canadensis
To 43 in. (1.1 m)

Wood Duck
Aix sponsa To 20 in. (50 cm)

Northern Pintail
Anas acuta To 29 in. (73 cm)

Blue-winged Teal
Spatula discors
To 16 in. (40 cm)

American Coot
Fulica americana
To 16 in. (40 cm)

Great Egret
Ardea alba
To 38 in. (95 cm)
Note yellow bill
and black feet.

Great Blue Heron
Ardea herodias
To 4.5 ft. (1.4 m)

Sandhill Crane
Antigone canadensis
To 4 ft. (1.2 m)

Double-crested Cormorant
Phalacrocorax auritus
To 3 ft. (90 cm)

Killdeer
Charadrius vociferus
To 12 in. (30 cm)
Note two breast bands.

American White Pelican
Pelecanus erythrorhynchos
To 5 ft. (1.5 m)

BIRDS

Ring-billed Gull
Larus delawarensis
To 20 in. (50 cm)
Bill has dark ring.

Franklin's Gull
Leucophaeus pipixcan
To 14 in. (35 cm)

Herring Gull
Larus argentatus
To 26 in. (65 cm)
Legs are pinkish.

Rock Pigeon
Columba livia
To 13 in. (33 cm)

Mourning Dove
Zenaida macroura
To 13 in. (33 cm)
Call is a mournful –
ooah-woo-woo-woo.

Wild Turkey
Meleagris gallopavo
To 4 ft. (1.2 m)

Northern Flicker
Colaptes auratus
To 13 in. (33 cm)
Wing and tail
linings are yellow.

Red-bellied Woodpecker
Melanerpes carolinus
To 11 in. (28 cm)

Hairy Woodpecker
Dryobates villosus
To 10 in. (25 cm)
The similar downy
woodpecker is
smaller and has
a shorter bill.

Barred Owl
Strix varia
To 2 ft. (60 cm)
Call is a loud –
"Who-cooks-for-
you? Who-cooks-
for-you-all?"

Bald Eagle
Haliaeetus leucocephalus
To 40 in. (1 m)

Osprey
Pandion haliaetus
To 2 ft. (60 cm)

Great Horned Owl
Bubo virginianus
To 25 in. (63 cm)
Call is a resonant –
hoo-HOO-hoooo.

Red-tailed Hawk
Buteo jamaicensis
To 25 in. (63 cm)

Broad-winged Hawk
Buteo platypterus
To 19 in. (48 cm)

Turkey Vulture
Cathartes aura
To 32 in. (80 cm)
Note red head.

BIRDS

Barn Swallow
Hirundo rustica
To 8 in. (20 cm)
Note deeply forked tail.

Tree Swallow
Tachycineta bicolor
To 6 in. (15 cm)

Blue Jay
Cyanocitta cristata
To 14 in. (35 cm)

Common Raven
Corvus corax
To 27 in. (68 cm)
Call is a hoarse croak.

American Crow
Corvus brachyrhynchos
To 22 in. (55 cm)
Call is a distinct – caw.

Red-winged Blackbird
Agelaius phoeniceus
To 9 in. (23 cm)

European Starling
Sturnus vulgaris
To 8 in. (20 cm)

Yellow-headed Blackbird
Xanthocephalus xanthocephalus
To 11 in. (28 cm)

Common Grackle
Quiscalus quiscula
To 14 in. (35 cm)

Black-capped Chickadee
Poecile atricapillus
To 6 in. (15 cm)
Name-saying call is –
chick-a-dee-dee-dee.

House Wren
Troglodytes aedon
To 5 in. (13 cm)

White-breasted Nuthatch
Sitta carolinensis
To 6 in. (15 cm)

Eastern Bluebird
Sialia sialis
To 7 in. (18 cm)

American Robin
Turdus migratorius
To 11 in. (28 cm)

Cedar Waxwing
Bombycilla cedrorum
To 7 in. (18 cm)
Red wing marks look
like waxy droplets.

BIRDS

Gray Catbird
Dumetella carolinensis
To 9 in. (23 cm)
Repetitive call of variable
sounds is interspersed
with cat-like mew notes.

Yellow Warbler
Setophaga petechia
To 5 in. (13 cm)

Yellow-rumped Warbler
Setophaga coronata
To 6 in. (15 cm)
Note yellow on rump
and crown and
white throat.

Common Yellowthroat
Geothlypis trichas
To 5 in. (13 cm)

Baltimore Oriole
Icterus galbula
To 8 in. (20 cm)

Dark-eyed Junco
Junco hyemalis
To 7 in. (18 cm)

Evening Grosbeak
Coccothraustes vespertinus
To 8 in. (20 cm)

Indigo Bunting
Passerina cyanea
To 6 in. (15 cm)

Song Sparrow
Melospiza melodia
To 7 in. (18 cm)
Note central
breast spot.

Rose-breasted Grosbeak
Pheucticus ludovicianus
To 9 in. (23 cm)

Scarlet Tanager
Piranga olivacea
To 7 in. (18 cm)

House Finch
Haemorhous mexicanus
To 6 in. (15 cm)

American Goldfinch
Spinus tristis
To 5 in. (13 cm)

Northern Cardinal
Cardinalis cardinalis
To 9 in. (23 cm)

Eastern Towhee
Pipilo erythrophthalmus
To 9 in. (23 cm)
Cheerful song is –
Drink-your-teeeeeeea!

MAMMALS

Virginia Opossum
Didelphis virginiana
To 40 in. (1 m)
Note long fur and naked tail.

Thirteen-lined Ground Squirrel
Spermophilus tridecemlineatus
To 12 in. (30 cm)

Little Brown Bat
Myotis lucifugus
To 3.5 in. (9 cm)

Fox Squirrel
Sciurus niger
To 28 in. (70 cm)
Note large size and
bushy tail. Largest
squirrel in the U.S.

Red Squirrel
Tamiasciurus hudsonicus
To 14 in. (35 cm)

Eastern Cottontail
Sylvilagus floridanus
To 18 in. (45 cm)

Eastern Chipmunk
Tamias striatus
To 12 in. (30 cm)
Note white stripes
on side and face.

Eastern Gray Squirrel
Sciurus carolinensis
To 20 in. (50 cm)

Common Porcupine
Erethizon dorsatum
To 3 ft. (90 cm)

Common Muskrat
Ondatra zibethicus
To 2 ft. (60 cm)
Aquatic rodent has
a naked tail that is
flattened on its sides.

Deer Mouse
Peromyscus maniculatus
To 8 in. (20 cm)
Distinguished by its white
undersides and hairy tail.

Woodchuck
Marmota monax
To 32 in. (80 cm)

American Badger
Taxidea taxus
To 35 in. (88 cm)

Common Raccoon
Procyon lotor To 40 in. (1 m)

Striped Skunk
Mephitis mephitis To 32 in. (80 cm)

American Beaver
Castor canadensis To 4 ft. (1.2 m)

MAMMALS

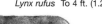

Northern River Otter
Lontra canadensis
To 52 in. (1.3 m)

Long-tailed Weasel
Mustela frenata To 21 in. (53 cm)
Note brown feet and yellowish neck.

Mink
Neovison vison
To 28 in. (70 cm)
Chin is white.

Common Gray Fox
Urocyon cinereoargenteus
To 3.5 ft. (1.1 m)
Note black-tipped tail.

Red Fox
Vulpes vulpes To 40 in. (1 m)
Note white-tipped tail.

Gray Wolf
Canis lupus To 6.5 ft. (2 m)
Coat color is usually gray, but black,
white and mottled variants exist.

Coyote
Canis latrans To 52 in. (1.3 m)
Note bushy, black-tipped tail.

Mountain Lion
Puma concolor To 9 ft. (2.7 m)

Black Bear
Ursus americanus
To 6 ft. (1.8 m)

Bobcat
Lynx rufus To 4 ft. (1.2 m)

Moose
Alces alces To 10 ft. (3 m)

White-tailed Deer
Odocoileus virginianus To 7 ft. (2 m)